4/25

BOOK ANALYSIS

By Elizabeth Smith

Dubliners

BY JAMES JOYCE

Bright
Summaries.com

BOOK ANALYSIS

Shed new light on your favorite books with

Bright
≡Summaries.com

www.brightsummaries.com

JAMES JOYCE 11

DUBLINERS 15

SUMMARY 19

- The Sisters
- An Encounter
- Araby
- Eveline
- After the Race
- Two Gallants
- The Boarding House
- A Little Cloud
- Counterparts
- Clay
- A Painful Case
- Ivy Day in the Committee Room
- A Mother
- Grace
- The Dead

CHARACTER STUDY 29

- The Sisters
- An Encounter
- Araby
- Eveline
- After the Race
- Two Gallants
- The Boarding House

A Little Cloud
Counterparts
Clay
A Painful Case
Ivy Day in the Committee Room
A Mother
Grace
The Dead

ANALYSIS 49

"Dear, dirty Dublin" (p. 63)
Religion
National identity
Marriage
Literary ambitions

FURTHER REFLECTION 57

FURTHER READING 61

JAMES JOYCE

IRISH NOVELIST, POET, AND SHORT STORY WRITER

- **Born in Dublin in 1882.**
- **Died in Zurich in 1941.**
- **Notable works:**
  - *A Portrait of the Artist as a Young Man* (1916), novel
  - *Ulysses* (1922), novel
  - *Finnegans Wake* (1939), novel

James Joyce was born into a financially unstable middle-class Irish Catholic family. He was the eldest of ten siblings, two of whom died. He studied at two Jesuit schools, then went to university in Dublin, before studying medicine in Paris. After giving up his degree, Joyce went home to be with his dying mother, but refused to kneel and pray at her deathbed. He met his future wife Nora Barnacle in 1904, although they did not marry until 1931. Joyce and Nora moved to Zurich, then Trieste, and had two children, George and

Lucia. Despite crippling eye problems, he built a reputation for himself as an avant-garde writer, often experimenting with stream-of-consciousness styles. Although Joyce gave up his Catholic faith, he continued to be influenced by religious imagery and ideas. He fled the Nazi occupation of France and moved back to Zurich in 1940, where he died after an operation in 1941.

DUBLINERS

SHORT STORY COLLECTION
FOLLOWING THE LIVES OF
EVERYDAY DUBLINERS

- **Genre:** short story collection
- **Reference edition:** Joyce, J (1992) *Dubliners*. London: Minerva.
- **1st edition:** 1914
- **Themes:** naturalism, everyday life, Irish nationalism, religion, the class system, marriage

Dubliners (1914) is a collection of 15 short stories on separate subjects that together build up a picture of the everyday dramas and hypocrisies of life for Dublin's middle classes. The stories reflect the anxieties of a period of social and political turbulence, with Irish nationalism on the rise. Joyce employs the relatively new technique of naturalism to capture the gritty and mundane details of everyday life. Joyce submitted *Dubliners* 18 times to 15 publishers, two of which came close to publishing but grappled with Joyce over censorship of some of the more scandalous episodes in the collection, before the collection was finally published by Grant Richards.

SUMMARY

THE SISTERS

This story focuses on a young boy who finds out that an old priest he was fond of, Father James Flynn, has died. His family did not approve of his closeness to the eccentric old man. They visit Nannie and Eliza, Flynn's relatives, who say that he was "crossed" (p. 9): after breaking a chalice and being found laughing in the confessional at night, he was never the same again and died a paralytic.

AN ENCOUNTER

Two boys decide to skip school to go on an adventure to the "Pigeon House" (p. 14), a Dublin landmark. While exploring the city, they encounter a strange man who talks to them about suggestive topics like sweethearts and whipping until they feel uncomfortable and decide to go home.

ARABY

A young boy, who lives with his uncle and aunt, is attracted to the sister of his friend Mangan. After she mentions that she would like to go to the bazar at Araby, but cannot, he asks his uncle to take him so he can bring her a gift. His uncle finds excuses to delay the trip, and eventually gives him money to go by himself. When he arrives, most of the stalls are closed, and he is intimidated by some judgemental English vendors. He goes home humiliated and empty-handed.

EVELINE

A young woman called Eveline seeks to escape her unhappy home life, where her father has been aggressive since her mother died and she is expected to manage the house. She plans to run away with a sailor called Frank, whom her father has forbidden her to see, and dreams of being respected as a wife. She is having doubts, however, and the story ends in a moment of indecision as Eveline pauses between boarding a ship with Frank and walking back to her old life.

AFTER THE RACE

Four young men enjoy the aftermath of a motor race. Jimmy Doyle, a college student known for his habits of excess, is enjoying the company of his wealthy and high-profile friends. He plans to invest in a financial scheme suggested by Ségouin. They spend the evening on a friend's yacht, where Jimmy loses money in a card game.

TWO GALLANTS

Lenehan and Corley are discussing Corley's affair with a servant-girl. Corley is exploiting the girl for money she is going to steal from her employer. Lenehan, a social leech, watches from a distance, jealous and alienated, as Corley succeeds in getting the money.

THE BOARDING HOUSE

Mrs Mooney, a strong-willed butcher's daughter whose husband became abusive after her father died, separates from him and opens a boarding house, housing tourists, music-hall performers, and clerks. Her daughter, Polly, who helps around the house, becomes involved with

Mr Doran, one of the guests. Mrs Mooney manoeuvres Doran into marrying Polly to save his reputation and her honour. Mr Doran suspects her of seeking an upwardly mobile marriage for her daughter, and the reader is left to decide on the outcome.

A LITTLE CLOUD

Chandler, regarded as "little" by his friends (p. 59), is going to meet his old friend Gallaher, who has made a name for himself in the London Press. Jealousy quickly surfaces over his own failed literary ambitions, as he feels himself superior to Gallaher. Gallaher, who was wilder in his youth, flaunts his knowledge of the world, including the "immoral" (p. 65) side of cities like Paris. There is some tension over the fact that Chandler is married but Gallaher is not: Gallagher views marriage as stale and confining. Back at home, Chandler's wife Annie is cold, and his baby will not stop crying. Feeling trapped by his family life, Chandler shouts at the child in frustration, but he quickly regrets this when Annie chastises him, and he feels hated by his wife and child.

COUNTERPARTS

Mr Farrington, a scrivener at a legal firm, has a difficult relationship with his boss, Mr Alleyne. He has not been meeting deadlines due to his alcoholism, and often goes out drinking in the middle of the day. He humiliates Alleyne with a sharp comeback in front of a wealthy client and potential love interest, and gloats about it to his friends in the pub later. Having already spent most of his money on alcohol, Farrington pawns his watch so he can go to the pub. The evening ends in bitterness when he fails to impress a woman he meets, fails to prove his manhood in an arm wrestling competition, and runs out of money. When he eventually stumbles home, he takes his frustration out by beating his son.

CLAY

Maria has the evening off from the laundry where she works so she can celebrate Hallows Eve with Joe, whom she raised. She enjoys buying cakes for the family, and strikes up a conversation with a gentleman on the train. Later, she discovers she has left one of the cakes behind. They play a traditional game and Maria feels self-conscious about being unmarried. Despite the rift in the family caused by Joe falling out with his brother Alphy, she enjoys the evening, and moves everyone by singing a nostalgic song.

A PAINFUL CASE

Mr James Duffy lives an orderly, passionless life. He is not in touch with his own body or with the life of the city. During his one luxury of visiting classical concerts, he meets a married woman, Mrs Emily Sinico, and they carry on a clandestine friendship, sharing books and ideas. James has quit the Irish Socialist Party, put off by its working class members and in-fighting, but still has faith in his own ideas. James and Emily become more intimate, but after Emily shows physical affection, James breaks their fellowship off in disgust, thinking it has been corrupted by sexual feelings. After going back to his dull life, James reads in the paper that Emily has been killed by a train, after succumbing to a life of alcoholism and loneliness. He is initially enraged by her immorality, but later wonders whether he condemned her to this end.

IVY DAY IN THE COMMITTEE ROOM

A group of men employed to canvas votes for a politician called Mr Tierney discuss corrupt politicians and church figures in the committee room with the old caretaker, Jack. Mr Tierney is yet to pay them, and some of the men suspect Mr Hynes of spying for the other candidate, although Mr O'Connor insists he is not. Tierney's moral fibre is called into question, and he fails to measure up with Parnell, a prominent Irish Nationalist whose death is commemorated on Ivy Day. The men drink stout, putting the bottles on the hob until the corks pop out, usually with comic timing. Hynes wears an ivy pin to show his respect for Parnell's memory, and he recites a poem he composed on the politician's death. Even Crofton, whose views are conservative, is moved by the poem.

A MOTHER

Mrs Kearney, a determined mother whose own romantic dreams were thwarted at a young age, tries to make a name for her daughter, Kathleen, as a musician in the Irish Revival movement. After Kathleen is invited to play as an accompanist for the *Eire Abu* society, Mrs Kearney draws up a contract. However, the concerts are poorly organised and the secretaries, Mr Holohan and Mr Fitzpatrick, are evasive. Afraid that her daughter will not be paid, Mrs Kearney creates chaos in the final performance by trying to stop her daughter from playing altogether. A replacement accompanist is found, however, and the family goes home in disgrace.

GRACE

Commercial traveller Tom Kernan injures himself by biting part of his tongue off after falling down some stairs while drunk at a bar. His friend, Mr Power, takes him home to his wife, and later persuades him to come to a religious retreat with some friends in an attempt to cure his alcoholism, despite the fact that Tom has previously neglected his faith. At church, the priest preaches a model of spiritual accountability based on financial accountancy, designed to appeal to modern businessmen.

THE DEAD

The sisters Kate and Julia Morkan, and their niece Mary Jane, are hosting a dance. All three of them are successful musicians, although the sisters are now quite elderly. Gabriel, a favourite nephew, is anxious about a speech he is expected to make over dinner and alarmed by his failed conversation with a young servant called Lily. The family struggles to manage the drunkenness of Freddy, another relative. Gabriel has an unsettling argument with his friend Miss Ivors over his lack of nationalist feeling: he writes for a notoriously "West Briton" (p. 169) newspaper and snaps about being sick of his own country. Miss Ivors leaves early and the speech is a success. As the guests leave in the early hours, Gabriel's wife, Ada, is lost in thought listening to an old Irish folk song. When they return to their hotel room, Gabriel is overcome with desire and love for Ada, but finds her sad and distracted. The song reminds her of a young man who died for love of her. This revelation depresses Gabriel, who looks out on the snow-covered landscape and dwells on the death of the young man, the wedge now driven between him and his wife, and his own future demise.

CHARACTER STUDY

THE SISTERS

Narrator

The narrator is a young boy who has formed a close attachment to the priest, Father Flynn, who has since died. Father Flynn taught him much, but his parents disapproved of their friendship because of the priest's reputation as an eccentric.

Father Flynn

According to his relatives, Father Flynn was "too scrupulous" (p. 8) for the priesthood, and he was later "crossed" (p. 9), deteriorating mentally after breaking a sacred chalice. While on his sickbed, Flynn takes the young boy under his wing.

AN ENCOUNTER

Narrator

The story is narrated by a young boy who enjoys playing cowboys and Indians, and decides to miss a day of school to go on an adventure with his friend Mahony. He is unsettled by an encounter with a strange old man.

Strange Man

Although Joyce never says so explicitly, it is implied that the strange old man is a paedophile, asking about corporal punishment and sweethearts to fuel his own fantasies.

ARABY

Narrator

A young boy becomes infatuated with the sister of his friend Mangan, which leads him to try – and fail – to go to the fair to bring something back for her.

Mangan's sister

Mangan's sister is an idealised figure, and we do not learn much about her character. She watches over her younger brother, and attends a convent school which is holding a religious retreat, preventing her from going to the fair.

Narrator's uncle

Although he raises the young boy, the uncle seems distracted and even dismissive at times, forgetting about his promise to take the boy to Araby.

EVELINE

Eveline

Eveline is a young woman who feels suffocated by her domestic obligations and threatened by her father. She plans to run away with Frank to win independence and respect as a married woman. She is uncertain about this decision, however.

Eveline's father

Eveline's father is a violent man, who has deteriorated since the death of his wife. He used to beat his sons when they were younger, and Eveline now fears that he will take to abusing her instead.

Frank

Frank is a "kind, manly, open-hearted" (p. 28) sailor who plans to whisk Eveline away to Buenos

Aires, even though Eveline's father disapproves of him.

AFTER THE RACE

Jimmy Doyle

Jimmy is a student at Cambridge, where he has met the wealthy Charles and his equally high-profile friends. He is well-off himself, and anxious to impress his new friends. This desire leads him to squander his money drinking and gambling, and even to invest in Charles' business venture.

Charles Ségouin

Charles is charming, wealthy, and powerful. He is embarking on a business venture selling motorcars, and lives the kind of glamorous lifestyle Jimmy aspires to.

TWO GALLANTS

Lenehan

Lenehan is a "leech" whose "eloquence" allows him to sponge money off his friends (p. 40). He shares a somewhat dubious moral code with his friend Corley, but he secretly envies Corley's love affair and toys with the idea of settling down with a family.

Corley

Corley is a self-absorbed, slightly ridiculous man who struggles to hold down the jobs his acquaintances get him. He has never had much luck with women, but brags throughout this story about his luck with the serving girl he has seduced, who produces a gold coin (presumably stolen from her employer) for him at the end of the story.

The girl

Since the focus of the story is on the two men and their treatment of her, the reader is not given many details about the serving girl Corley has seduced. She has a "blunt" and "healthy" (p. 45) appearance, and seems to think Corley is a gentleman who is more committed than he really is.

THE BOARDING HOUSE

Mrs Mooney

Mrs Mooney is a strong-willed woman who has separated from her abusive, drunkard husband and sold her butcher's shop to open a boarding house, which she runs firmly and efficiently. When she notices that her daughter has become entangled with one of the guests, she does not act immediately, and later manoeuvres both parties into a marriage which will elevate her daughter socially, using the young man's reputation as leverage.

Polly

Polly is an attractive, flirtatious girl who falls for Bob Doran, one of the guests at the boarding house. After her mother finds out and intervenes, she is distressed, but this feeling is overwhelmed by her hopes for a better life.

Bob Doran

Bob Doran is in a crisis of indecision throughout the story, knowing that he must save his reputation and his soul by marrying Polly, yet resentful of being manipulated by Mrs Mooney, and anxious that he will lose his freedom. He can imagine a comfortable life with Polly, however, and eventually agrees to marry her.

A LITTLE CLOUD

Chandler

Nicknamed "little" (p. 59) Chandler due to an air of smallness he has about him, Chandler has stayed behind in Dublin while his old friend Gallaher has made his fortune in the London Press. Although pleased to see Gallaher, he is jealous of his success and secretly thinks himself more deserving of fame, as the more educated of the two. He views himself as a poet in the making, and curses his own inability to follow through on his literary ambitions. Meanwhile, his wife has grown cold towards him and he resents her and his baby for holding him back from success.

Gallaher

Gallaher left Dublin after a wild youth and has made a name for himself in the London Press. He prides himself on his experience of the world and his knowledge of both the "gay" and the "immoral" (p. 65) side of cities like Paris. He has fallen out of touch with Chandler. Gallaher bitterly implies that Chandler is held back by his marriage, and declares that he will never let himself be tied town, unless he does so for money.

Annie

Chandler never shares his literary ambitions or his love of poetry with his wife Annie, who is disappointed at his lack of attention to domestic details like buying tea. She is "ladylike" but seems "mean" (p. 71) to Chandler, and is fiercely protective of their baby, who is beginning to supplant Chandler in her affections.

COUNTERPARTS

Mr Farrington

Mr Farrington lives from drink to drink, and his pay from his job as a scrivener at a legal firm is scarcely enough to cover his habit. His boss, Mr Alleyne, is furious with him over his poor-quality work and frequent trips to the pub at lunchtime.

Mr Farrington takes his insecurities and frustrations out on his wife and children, beating his son at the end of the story.

Mr Alleyne

Mr Alleyne bears a grudge towards Mr Farrington, an unreliable employee who once made fun of his Northern Irish accent. His rage reaches its climax when Mr Farrington humiliates him in front of Miss Delacour, a wealthy woman he is trying to impress.

CLAY

Maria

Maria is a small, unmarried woman working in a laundry run by Protestants (despite being Catholic herself), where she is well regarded as a "peace-maker" (p. 86). She is very fond of the two brothers she nursed, Joe and Alphy, although they have fallen out and will no longer acknowledge each other. Despite enjoying her independence, Maria sometimes catches herself longing for married life.

Joe

Except for those occasions when he drinks too much, Joe is a merry family man. After fighting with Alphy, he refuses to acknowledge him as a brother.

A PAINFUL CASE

Mr James Duffy

Living "a little distance from his body" (p. 94), Mr James Duffy is idealistic but repulsed by all things physical. His otherwise spartan shell of routine permits him to go to classical music concerts, where he meets Emily, a married woman with whom he quickly becomes close. He was once a member of the Irish Socialist Party, but quit because of the in-fighting and what he saw as a repellent fixation of the working men with wages. James enjoys her companionship and showing off his intellect to her, but he is horrified when Emily tries to make their passion physical. Years after breaking off the friendship and settling back into his old routine, James reacts to Emily's death first with repulsion, then with regret for condemning them both to a life of loneliness.

Mrs Emily Sinico

Mrs Emily Sinico is an intelligent and self-willed woman who shares James' passion for classical music. She has a grown-up daughter and a husband who is the captain of a mercantile boat. She and James are drawn together by their loneliness, and the chance to connect emotionally and intellectually. When Emily tries to take their attachment to a physical level, however, she is rejected by James. Her subsequent decline into alcoholism culminates in her death while crossing a railway line.

IVY DAY IN THE COMMITTEE ROOM

Mr O'Connor

Appearing older than his years, O'Connor approaches his job with cynicism. He insists on seeing the best in Hynes, however.

Old Jack

The aged caretaker of the Committee premises is friendly with the canvassers who come and go, but liable to be grumpy and suspicious. He mistrusts Hynes, and struggles with his rebellious teenage son.

Mr Hynes

Hynes is a young and somewhat enigmatic friend of O'Connor, suspected by Jack of spying for the other candidate, due to his financial difficulties. Hynes wears an ivy leaf on his lapel in support of Charles Stuart Parnell, a prominent and much-mourned member of the Irish Nationalist Party. He harbours literary ambitions, and the story closes with his impassioned verse on Parnell's death.

Mr Crofton

Mr Crofton is a self-important canvasser who used to work for the conservative candidate.

Father Keon

The canvassers treat Father Keon with respect when he is present, but they privately suspect him of being corrupt. This cynicism extends to the church in general.

Mr Henchy

Henchy is a bustling little man with outspoken views about the state of politics and religion in Ireland, who is convinced that Hynes is spying for the opposition. Broke and unpaid, he has very little faith in the candidate he represents, but a lot of faith in his own abilities as a canvasser.

A MOTHER

Mrs Kearney

Another determined woman, Mrs Kearney traded her girlhood dreams of romance for motherhood. She tries to organise her daughter Kathleen's career in music, and hosts gatherings of musicians and Irish National revivals. When Kathleen is invited to play the piano in a series of concerts for the *Eire Abu* society, Mrs Kearney grapples with the disorganised Mr Holohan and Mr Fitzpatrick to ensure that Kathleen gets paid, and even draws up a contract. Her intervention backfires when she halts the concert to demand payment, Kathleen is replaced by another pianist, and they are forced to leave.

Kathleen

Kathleen is mostly happy to defer to her overbearing mother, and takes a back seat in her own musical career.

Mr Holohan

Mr Holohan is assistant secretary for the *Eire Abu* society, and is organising a series of concerts. After he enlists Kathleen as an accompanist, Mrs Kearney starts to take over. He is hopelessly disorganised, and tries to deflect Mrs Kearney by passing responsibility onto first Mr Fitzpatrick, then the committee (a committee Mrs Kearney believes to be an invention).

Mr Fitzpatrick

To Mrs Kearney, Mr Fitzpatrick, the secretary of the society, seems careless and unprofessional. Like Mr Holohan, he sidesteps responsibility for the organisation of the concerts and Kathleen's payment.

Mr Kearney

Mrs Kearney uses her husband as a stage prop and token male presence in her negotiations with Mr Holohan and Mr Fitzpatrick. He is dependable, but mostly overshadowed by his wife.

GRACE

Tom Kernan

When we first meet him, Tom Kernan has fallen down the lavatory stairs at a bar where he has been drinking heavily. He is an old-fashioned commercial trader. Although tolerated by his long-suffering wife, his alcoholism has become bad enough for his friends to intervene by inviting him to rediscover his faith, which he had neglected after converting to Catholicism some years before.

Mr Power

Mr Power is the first to intervene when Tom has his accident, and the mastermind of the retreat. He is employed by the Constabulary, and is "debonair" with "surprising debts" (p. 137).

Mrs Kernan

Mr and Mrs Kernan have just celebrated their silver wedding anniversary, and Mrs Kernan still remembers the romance of marrying a very different man. Her sons are well established in careers, however, and Mrs Kernan has put up with her husband's intemperance up to this point.

Mr Cunningham

Martin Cunningham, a colleague of Power's, does most of the talking during the intervention. His wife is apparently a drunkard who keeps pawning the furniture, and everyone respects him as a sensible man with a lot of life experience.

THE DEAD

Kate Morkan

Kate and Julia are the hostesses of an annual dance. They were both professional musicians, and are still prolific at the time of the party, although much older. Kate is the more vivacious of the two.

Julia Morkan

Julia has aged worse than her sister, but she still sings beautifully, performing to rapturous applause at her own party.

Mary Jane

Now a successful music teacher, Mary Jane grew up under the instruction of her aunts.

Lily

Lily, the caretaker's daughter, works for Kate and Julia. She has recently been acting up and reacts badly to Gabriel's comment about boyfriends.

Gabriel Conroy

Kate and Julia's favourite nephew is kind-hearted but anxious about his education getting between him and people like Lily. He indulges his love of reading and writing by submitting articles to the *Daily Press*, which he does not see as political, despite the allegations of Miss Ivors. He is baffled by Miss Ivors's determined nationalism and fed up with his country. His passion and deep affection for his wife is complicated by an unexpected revelation at the end of the story.

Gretta Conroy

Gabriel's wife, Gretta, has been hiding the secret of her love affair with a young man who died for her. When it resurfaces after the party, she is thrown into emotional turmoil, and finally tells her husband about it.

Miss Ivors

Miss Ivors is a determinedly nationalist friend who challenges Gabriel over his apparent lack of patriotism.

ANALYSIS

"DEAR, DIRTY DUBLIN" (P. 63)

Joyce uses naturalism, a literary technique characterised by precise observation, detached narrators, and determinism, to attend to the everyday. Stories like 'Two Gallants' offer an insight into the more grimy and morally questionable sides of Dublin life, to the displeasure of several publishers. The bleakly repetitive routines of daily life can be erosive, as seen in the "life of commonplace sacrifices" (p. 29) of Eveline's mother. Perhaps seeking escape from this routine, many of Joyce's characters turn to alcoholism, particularly in 'Counterparts' and 'Grace'. However, characters like Mr James Duffy, who try to avoid the "dirty" side of Dublin, are portrayed as living stale lives. The everyday, somewhat scandalous underbelly of Dublin is nonetheless more alive than the cold, clinical alternative, and there may be a hint of affection beneath Joyce's otherwise ambivalent narratorial tone. Ironically, however, "dear, dirty Dublin" is so labelled by Gallaher, an outsider who has forsaken his home city for London.

RELIGION

Religion is a presence across many of these stories, but it is rarely presented in a positive light. Most of the priests in the story are either odd and disreputable like Father Flynn in 'The Sisters', or suspected of corruption like Father Keen in 'Ivy Day in the Committee Room'. The one effective religious figure is Father Purdon of 'Grace', who approaches spirituality through an economic lens. He preaches salvation as a balancing of "accounts" (p. 156) in order to appeal to an audience of businessmen. However, this pairing of religion and money casts the sermon in a dubious light. As in many of Joyce's other works, such as *A Portrait of the Artist as a Young Man*, religion is a point of political contention. This controversy was due in part to the Catholic church's public condemnation of the Irish Nationalist politician Charles Stuart Parnell after a scandal, which many believed led to his death.

NATIONAL IDENTITY

National identity is also at issue in *Dubliners*, a collection that proclaims its strong connection to place from the title to its frequent Dublin place names. Although in 'Araby' the Englishness of the market sellers is a tool to intimidate and embarrass the young narrator, the Irish Nationalist cause is not presented in a uniformly positive light either. In 'A Little Cloud', Chandler's efforts to seem more Irish as a poet are humorously shallow, and Mrs Kearney of 'A Mother' seems to invite Nationalist guests to improve her family's social standing. The death of Parnell, a prominent figure in the Irish Nationalist Party, is commemorated by Hynes's poem in 'Ivy Day in the Committee Room'. Although the memory of Parnell commands respect in that story, however, this only serves to expose the failings of the political climate in which the canvassers work. Frustrated by the accusations of the patriotic Miss Ivors, Gabriel snaps and exclaims: "I'm sick of my own country" (p. 170). Gabriel's insistence that his writing for an anti-nationalist newspaper is not political can be seen as naïve. However, his conflicted feelings towards his country may reflect Joyce's own. The writer himself oscillated between trying to embrace his cultural heritage by taking classes in the Irish language, and living in a self-imposed exile from his home country.

MARRIAGE

In line with the universal failure of human relationships in *Dubliners*, marriage is rarely a matter of genuine connection. For men like Mr Doran of 'The Boarding House' and Chandler from 'A Little Cloud', marriage is a matter of confinement. Mr Doran suspects he has been "had" (p. 56) by Polly's family, but is forced to go along with it for the sake of his reputation. After his friend Gallagher implies that being married must get "stale" (p. 70), Chandler begins to think of himself as a "prisoner for life" (p. 72), trapped by his family. Joyce also offers us the female perspective on this confinement, however. Eveline plans to win respect and independence for herself through marriage, despite the fact that marriage trapped her mother in a "life of commonplace sacrifices" and domesticity (p. 29). *Dubliners* is full of mistreated wives, who are forced to put up with alcoholic and abusive husbands. As one of very few options available to women in 20th-century Dublin, marriage can also offer social betterment. Mrs Mooney hopes it will improve the social status of her daughter Polly in 'The Boarding House', even though she herself split from her abusive husband.

LITERARY AMBITIONS

Three of Joyce's protagonists have literary ambitions, but none of them are presented in an unequivocally positive light. In 'A Little Cloud', Chandler muses that he has the soul of a poet and mentally tortures himself for his lack of success. He sees writing as a way of asserting himself in the world, and feels bitter that Gallaher, who he sees as inferior, has succeeded in the London Press. Chandler blames his family for holding him back from achieving literary fame, but takes no action to further his own career. Hynes of 'Ivy Day in the Committee Room' is suspected of spying on his friends, but manages to redeem himself with a poem written about Parnell's death. In 'The Dead', Gabriel writes literary articles for a newspaper. Although he writes out of a genuine enthusiasm for books, Gabriel's insistence that politics have nothing to do with it strikes the reader as naïve. Gabriel refuses to acknowledge that writing engages with the political world, and for Chandler life gets between him and his literary pretensions. Hynes's poetry may have hit its mark, but his character is called into question by the rest of the story. In all three cases, there is a mismatch between the writer's ideals and the effect of their writing. Perhaps this ambivalent presentation reflects the personal anxieties of a writer who was so frequently rejected by publishers, and who struggled against the political divisions of his country.

FURTHER REFLECTION

SOME QUESTIONS TO THINK ABOUT...

- Can religion offer any solace in Joyce's Dublin?
- The subjects of the stories seem to get progressively older throughout the collection, from childhood to maturity. Why do you think Joyce chose to arrange them like this?
- Why is alcoholism so prevalent in *Dubliners*? Are the characters escaping from something in their everyday lives?
- Does Joyce represent Irish nationalism positively, negatively, or ambivalently?
- Among the many misunderstandings and thwarted relationships of *Dubliners*, is there any possibility for genuine human connection?
- How should we react to the moments of antisemitism in some of the stories? Do they reflect the characters, or the author?
- Why do you think Joyce switches between first- and third-person narration between stories?

- *Dubliners* was refused publication several times because some of the stories were seen as morally shocking. Do you think this is a reflection of a hypocritical society, unable to confront its own contradictions?

*We want to hear from you!
Leave a comment on your online library
and share your favourite books on social media!*

FURTHER READING

REFERENCE EDITION

- Joyce, J (1992) *Dubliners*. London: Minerva.

REFERENCE STUDIES

- Bulson, E. (2006) *The Cambridge Introduction to James Joyce*. Cambridge: Cambridge University Press.

ADDITIONAL SOURCES

- Ayers, D. (2004) *Modernism: A Short Introduction*. Oxford: Blackwell.
- Bowers, G. (2012) *James Joyce: A New Biography*. New York: Farrar.

ADAPTATIONS

- *Dublin One*. (1963) [Play]. Hugh Leonard. Gate Theatre, Dublin.

MORE FROM BRIGHTSUMMARIES.COM

- Reading guide – *A Portrait of the Artist as a Young Man* by James Joyce.
- Reading guide – *Ulysses* by James Joyce.

Bright
≡Summaries.com

More guides to rediscover your love of literature

Animal Farm
BY GEORGE ORWELL

The Stranger
BY ALBERT CAMUS

Harry Potter and the Sorcerer's Stone
BY J.K. ROWLING

The Silence of the Sea
BY VERCORS

Antigone
BY JEAN ANOUILH

The Flowers of Evil
BY BAUDELAIRE

www.brightsummaries.com

Although the editor makes every effort to verify the accuracy of the information published, BrightSummaries.com accepts no responsibility for the content of this book.

© BrightSummaries.com, 2019. All rights reserved.

www.brightsummaries.com

Ebook EAN: 9782808015875

Paperback EAN: 9782808015882

Legal Deposit: D/2018/12603/553

Cover: © Primento

Digital conception by Primento, the digital partner of publishers.